Contemporary
Textured Surfaces
in Fabric and Thread

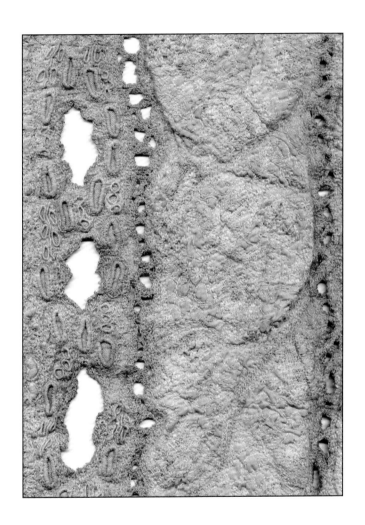

by Margaret Talbot

TEAMWORK
CRAFTBOOKS

Contemporary Textured Surfaces
in Fabric and Thread

First published in 2017 by Teamwork Craftbooks

Text, photographs and stitchery © Margaret Talbot
Illustrations © Gail Lawther

ISBN 978-1-9998035-2-0

British Library Cataloguing in Publication Data
A catalogue record for this book is available from the British Library

Designed by Teamwork, Christopher and Gail Lawther
100 Wiston Avenue, Worthing, West Sussex, BN14 7PS
e-mail: thelawthers@ntlworld.com   website: www.gaillawther.co.uk

Printed by Gemini Print, Unit A1, Dolphin Way, Shoreham-by-Sea, West Sussex BN43 6NZ

Contents

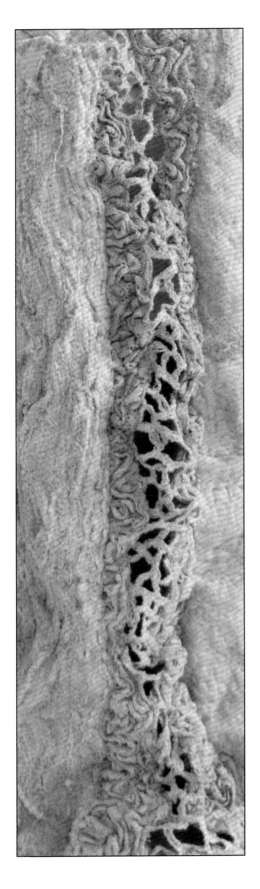

Definitions

Texture:

'A visual and especially tactile quality of a surface.'

'The characteristic structure of the interwoven or intertwined threads, strands, or the like, that make up a textile fabric.'

'An essential or characteristic quality; essence.'

'The nature of the surface other than smooth.'

Introduction

Most natural surfaces are textured, especially when you view them under a microscope; the variety is endless, and fascinating. Texture adds so much to a created item, providing interest and a tactile quality to the surface, and this is something that is fairly easy to achieve in textiles. Studying different surfaces is a never-ending source of inspiration; my constant aim is to create a gloriously tactile and incredibly fascinating surface in my work.

No matter what your ability or level of expertise, I hope that this book will inspire you to include a variety of hand and machine techniques for your work, resulting in many and varied textured surfaces. On the following pages I'll show you many different ways to create contemporary textured surfaces, using mainly natural fabrics and cotton thread. The natural fabrics could include scraps of silk, cotton, calico, scrim and muslin, plus pieces of cotton lace or crochet from old household linen (such as table runners and chair-backs). It's always useful to have a variety of white hand-sewing threads of different thickness and textures, and also machine thread that is 100% cotton: man-made fabrics and threads don't take up any dye or colouring in the same way.

Equipment is minimal, and you don't need any mixed media or coloured fabrics – my examples have mostly been made in white and cream fabrics and thread, and dyed afterwards – but there's no reason why you can't include coloured pieces from the start if you wish.

When you've completed your work, the piece can be dyed if you like, or just dipped into tea, and will still remain soft. Using one colour range – as I do through most of this book – helps both you and the viewer to focus on the texture and the shadows cast by the manipulation. I hope that this book inspires you to do some research of your own, and also experiment – to create new surfaces which give pleasure.

Texture

Texture adds so much extra interest to a piece of work; it can be created by hand or machine, using a wide variety of methods. Layering, padding, cords, and fabric manipulation (which includes ruching, pleating and gathering), when you do them creatively, can all build sculptured, embossed and unusual textured surfaces. You can also vary the effects by working at different scales; for instance, a technique such as ruching or gathering can be fine and regular, or large and uneven – or a mixture! Cords, manipulated fabrics and sculptural stitching are some of the other ways in which you can alter the surface of your work, and I also recommend beads and stumpwork for adding extra variety.

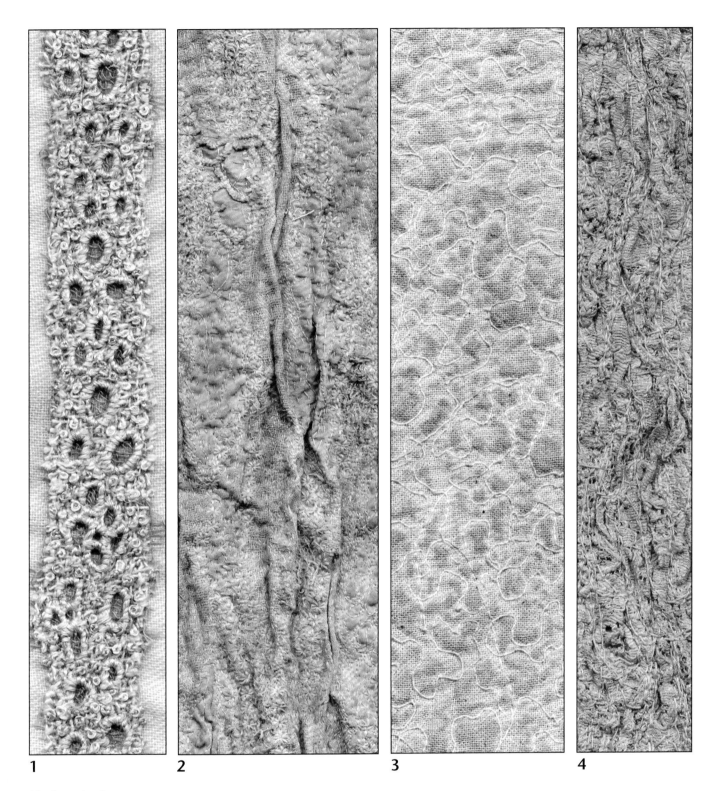

1 **2** **3** **4**

Various textures

1 Pulled work with French knots

2 An already-textured surface, gathered to create extra interest

3 A layered lace sandwich

4 Ruching

Rock formations: Petra, Jordan

When I was studying the rocks I was fascinated by the eroded surfaces, which left holes exposing layers – these created an intriguing variety of shapes.

Inspiration

You can just sit down and start playing and experimenting with fabric and thread, but I often find that I need a particular inspiration to kick-start a project. While I was on holiday a while ago I visited and photographed the caves and rocks of Petra in Jordan, Cappodocia in Turkey and Matera in Italy. I soon became fascinated by the rock formations. I studied the rock layers and the edges, the folds, crevices and worn surfaces: some were smooth and some rough, and there was often a mixture of surfaces that disappeared and then re-emerged further along a particular rock-face. Rocks are so varied in texture, scale and form that they will be a never-ending source of inspiration for my raised and textured surfaces.

As inspiration for your own projects, try looking around at the natural world: leaves, stones, flowers, water, clouds … Start a scrapbook, and if you see an interesting image or texture in a magazine or brochure, tear or cut that swatch out and stick it in your scrapbook. Jot down words to describe the image, such as gritty, cracked, wrinkled, lumpy … Similarly, when you come across a beautifully-textured yarn or an intriguing piece of lace, pop it in a bag or a folder alongside your scrapbook. When you're next looking for ideas to explore, you'll have a whole batch ready at your fingertips.

I enjoy experimenting with fabric, and being surprised by what can be achieved by altering and manipulating the surface. After years of machine work, computer textile design and using mixed media, I find it quite relaxing to use just a needle, thread and fabric. Although I still do some machining, the manipulation and construction have to be done by hand.

Rock formations: Petra, Jordan

A raking light helps to emphasise the different layers and shapes of textured pieces – keep this idea in mind when you're photographing your own work.

Design

Once you have been inspired by a subject it can be very tempting to translate your image quite literally. Make the subject your own by trying out various designs before choosing how to interpret it into embroidery. Capture the essence and feel of the subject, and find a method of making it different or unusual; exaggerate or reduce areas to give a range of different sizes. I find that it helps to jot down words; do this for your topic of inspiration, then refer back to them frequently when you're evaluating your work. For instance, you might have written down words such as:

weathered	*flowing*
fragile	*crumbling*
blended	*contrasting.*

Then you can ask yourself if you've captured these concepts. Don't try and include too many different effects on the same piece, as this can be confusing: the work needs to be unified. By all means use lots of different textures, but they should blend to give a seamless flow and rhythm to the work. One way you can achieve this is by linking or overlapping stitches from one texture to another. If you want to include areas of heavy manipulation along with finer textures, give plenty of thought to how you can do this successfully, and try some experiments first on a small scale. Consider the work as a whole, and refer back frequently to your design source(s).

Rock Climb *20cm (h) x 16cm (w) (above)* and **Rock Sculpture** *20cm (h) x 26cm (w) (right)*
These two sculptures were made from a machine-quilted piece of work which included sections of sewn-down crochet thread. I cut the work up into sections, then manipulated and joined them to create various shapes.

3D Construction

For 3D work the fabric needs to be firm enough to hold its shape. I prefer not to use wire, card or anything other than fabric in my work; wrapping, gathering, ruching, pleating and quilting can all be self-supporting, especially where the fabric has been manipulated several times – that creates a very firm fabric which is usually sufficient to hold a particular shape. When you sandwich wadding in between layers and stitch closely by machine, you can create a firm base or lining which can be for all kinds of constructions. Rolled or tightly twisted fabric can also be used to create supports, then covered with a top layer.

Cords – Machine-Stitched and Hand-Stitched

Cords can be joined to form a fabric, and are often used for making 3D items such as pots, baskets or bowls; their versatility for forming different shapes is very useful. You can also bunch them together to form thicker forms, plait them, or couch them down on a base fabric.

Machine-wrapped cords

For the core of the cord, use a single thick thread, several finer threads, or a narrow strip of fabric. Set your sewing machine for free machining, and select a wide satin stitch. Hold the threads or fabric strip firmly behind and in front of the machine foot, and stitch down the length of the core; this will bind the different elements together. Keep the cord taut, and you can move the strip backwards and forwards as required, filling in any gaps in the stitching.

Hand-wrapped cords

You can wrap torn strips of fabric or a bunch of threads with all kinds of other threads, working either randomly or at regular intervals. Textured yarns add extra interest. If the threads resist being wound around the core, use a needle and fine thread to secure them in place either visibly or invisibly. Lace or hand embroidery stitches can also be used to add extra texture to the outside of a cord.

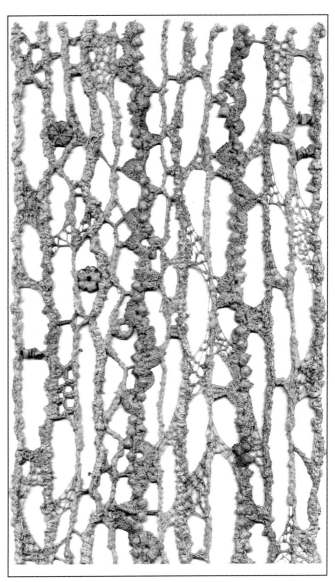

Thick cords

The first two examples show cords wrapped with different laces; the third is what I call a 'feature cord,' on which I've included all kinds of different textures.

Cords joined with needle-lace

I tacked firm-textured cords onto a laminated A4 sheet to create a framework for added needle-lace (see page 31) and beads.

Pleats and Gathers

These techniques aren't usually associated with embroidery – they're more commonly associated with dressmaking – but if they're finely worked, both pleats and gathers can add texture and interest to your work.

Gathered Pleats

First make a fold in the fabric horizontally, and machine close to the edge all the way across (**a**). Make another fold a little further down and machine across in the same way (**b**); continue until you have the fabric filled with horizontal ridges (**c**). Take a substantial needle and very strong machine thread; at the back of the work, secure the thread tightly at the beginning of the stitching line, then work running stitch by hand across the back. Leave a length of thread at the end of the row for gathering (**d**). Continue working down the length of the fabric with separate rows of running stitch (**e**); when they are all complete, draw up the free ends at the end of the rows to gather the work randomly as shown (**f**). Secure the loose threads firmly.

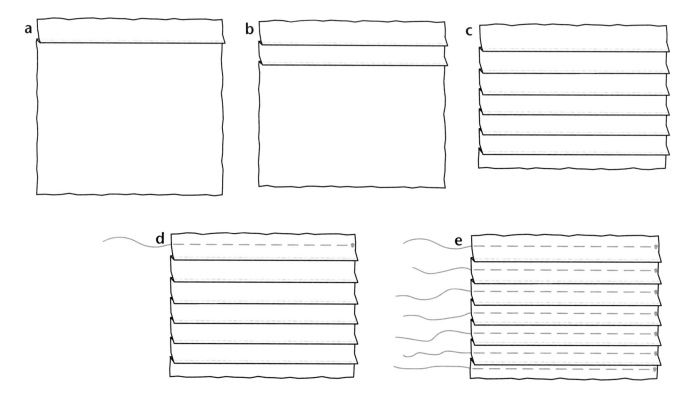

Irregular Gathering

To create an irregular effect, use a strong thread to work lines of running stitch either across the fabric (**a**) or lengthwise. Leave the thread loose at the end of each row; when you've worked your way across the whole piece of work (**b**), draw the threads up to create the effect you want – the size of the stitches and the gap between the rows will affect the outcome of the texture (**c**).

c

a
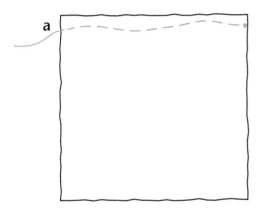

b
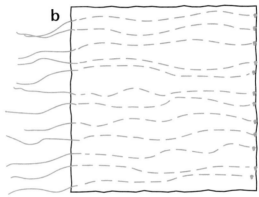

Horizontal and Diagonal Pleats

For this piece I first of all embellished the ground fabric with decorative machine stitching, and thin strips of lace running horizontally (**a**). I then pleated the fabric diagonally, and machine-stitched along the pleat edges (**b**). Finally, I created a second set of pleats in the opposite direction to the first set, and again machine stitched them (**c**). This kind of manipulation on top of manipulation requires the fabric to be quite fine to start with, as each process makes the fabric less pliable.

a
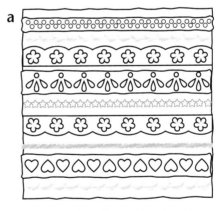

c
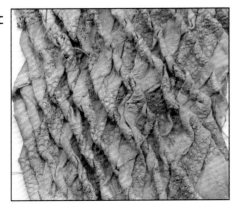

b
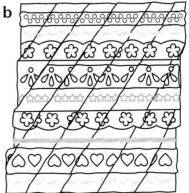

Pleats and Gathers

Narrow strips of lace, folded and hand-sewn together

Fine lace machined onto thin cotton; I then worked lines of hand running stitch and drew up the ends to form irregular gathers

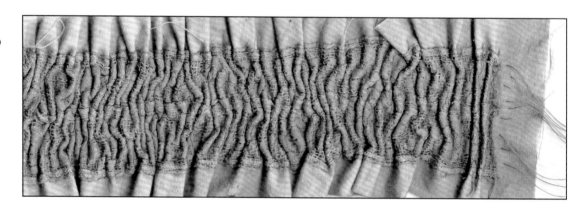

Ricrac braid folded into a tube ready for manipulating

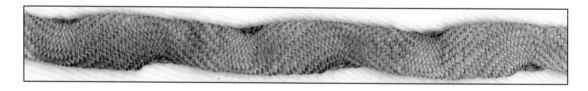

Combined techniques, including manipulated ricrac, couched yarns, folded lace and cords

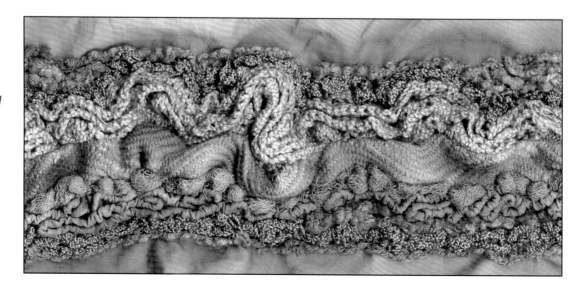

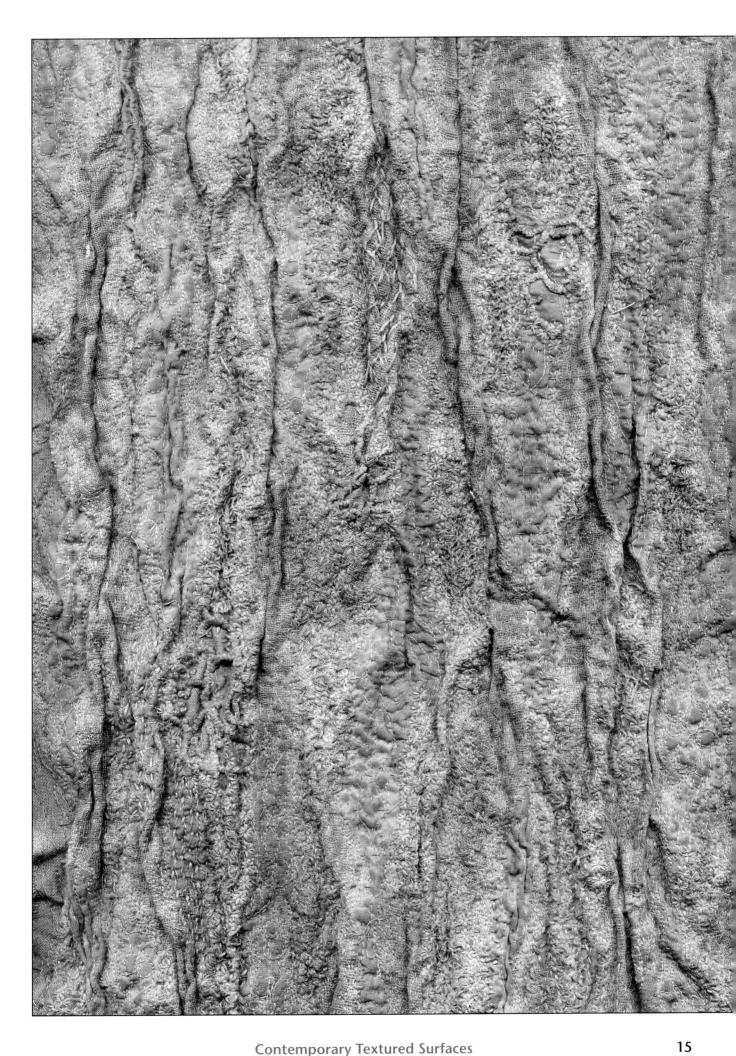

Ruching by Hand

Ruching is gathering fabric into informal tucks. It works best when it's done with fine fabric for the top layer, and a ground fabric of medium-weight cotton or calico. Work the stitches with a fine thread and needle; these stitches hold the fabric in place without being seen. First of all, secure the fine top fabric with a stab stitch to the ground fabric, then use the needle to push a small amount of the fabric to create texture, and secure with another stitch. Continue in the same way, but vary the directions in which the fabric is gathered so that the surface looks completely random. The stitches will be hidden in the creases between the ridges.

For a much bolder look use a thicker top fabric. This can be pre-textured to add interest, perhaps with lines of machine patterns or hand seeding. Secure the top fabric with a back-stitch to the ground fabric, and pinch a small adjacent section; again, secure with a back-stitch. Continue like this, pinching and sewing at different angles to produce a random effect. You can also add beads or work embroidery stitches into the depressions for added interest or contrast.

Ruching can also be done in a formal way by drawing a grid pattern on the back of the fabric and connecting the corners with a strong thread; for instance, for the sample far right I drew a square pattern on the back of the fabric, then picked up each point with a small stitch and pulled the thread taut.

Fine hand-ruching

Ruching and fabric manipulation

Random ruching, combined with pulled work (right)

Ruching and fabric manipulation (below) – pinching and sewing, as described on page 16

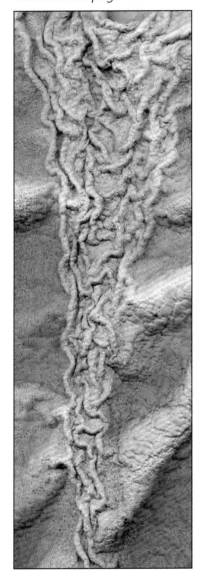

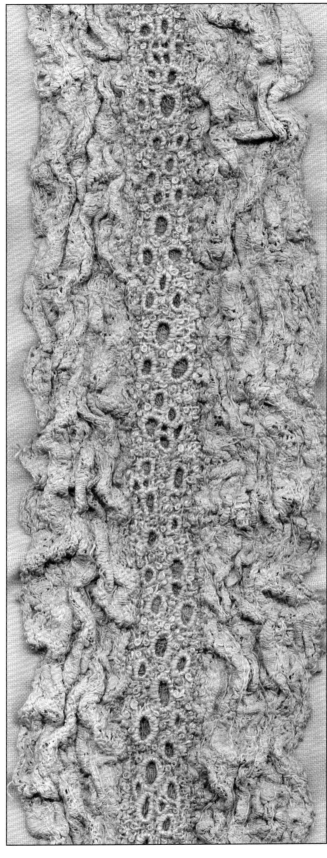

Formal ruching, gathered by stitching through a grid marked on the back of the fabric

Water Run *vessel*
34cm (h) x 13cm (w)

Faggoting

Insertion stitches – or faggoting – are used to join two pieces of fabric across a gap to create a decorative seam. This can be done by hand or machine, but whichever you are doing, the edges of the fabric must be firm – either hemmed, or satin stitched.

Working by machine

Pin the two edges to be joined onto a long strip of soluble fabric, leaving the required gap (**a**); pinning the pieces this way keeps the gap consistent. Using free machining and straight stitch, machine to and fro across the gap about 6 or 8 times for stability, with each line of stitching exactly on top of the previous ones (**b**). Then, move along the gap to the next place where you want to create a crossing (**c**). I find that it works best for this technique to choose a style and keep to it – for example, straight across at intervals (**d**), or slanted or V shapes (**e**), or circles (**f**). Cut any excess soluble fabric away from the back of the work, and dissolve the rest in warm water to leave the faggoting stitches (**g**).

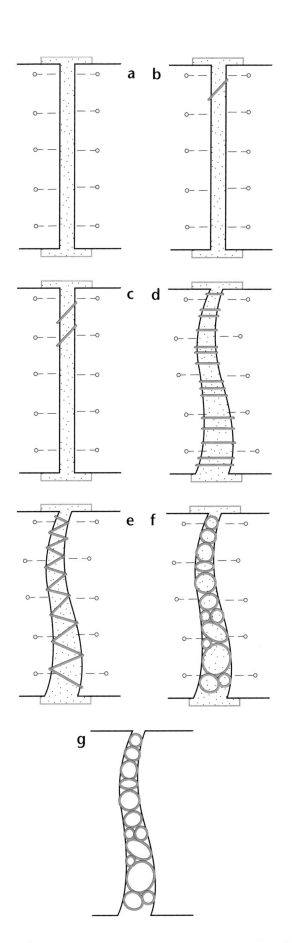

Working by hand

Pin the two edges in place to create a gap as above, but this time using a long strip of paper behind them (**a**). There are numerous insertion stitches you can choose from to create the faggoting, for instance herringbone, Cretan stitch, zigzag chain stitch, feather stitch to name just a few; page through a dictionary of embroidery stitches for ideas. Once the stitching is complete, unpin the paper (**b**).

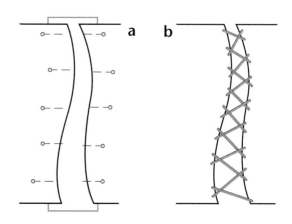

Being able to see through the top layer of work, and perhaps to see a contrasting layer underneath, adds another dimension to your work. When the faggoting is complete, it can be manipulated into waves or folds, and small sections can be inserted into other textures for added interest. Laced or beaded stitches can also look very attractive.

Styles of machine faggoting

In the bottom example, I've combined machine faggoting with ruching

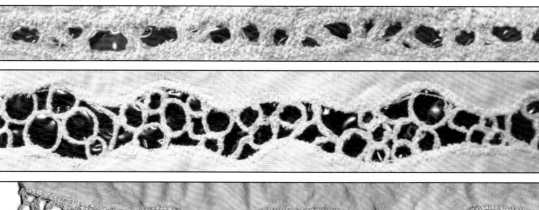

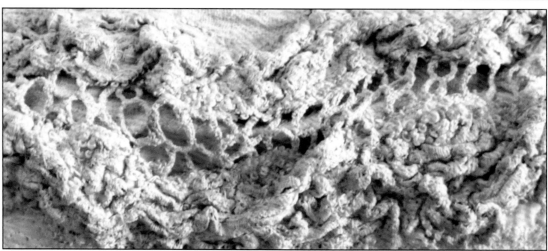

Recycling

Old lace

Lace and crochet can add some wonderful textures. Look for old chair-backs, table runners or broderie anglaise fabrics – particularly the thicker cotton pieces, as these will give an embossed look to the work. Cut them into small pieces and machine the pieces either onto soluble fabric, or onto a ground fabric of cotton; use cotton thread, so that it will blend in when you're dyeing the fabric. For the first sample (overleaf), I used broderie anglaise flowers, rearranging them and positioning them closely so that there are no gaps between the sections. I then machined the pieces into place. I used the same technique with the broderie anglaise edges (overleaf), laying them down to form a wave pattern.

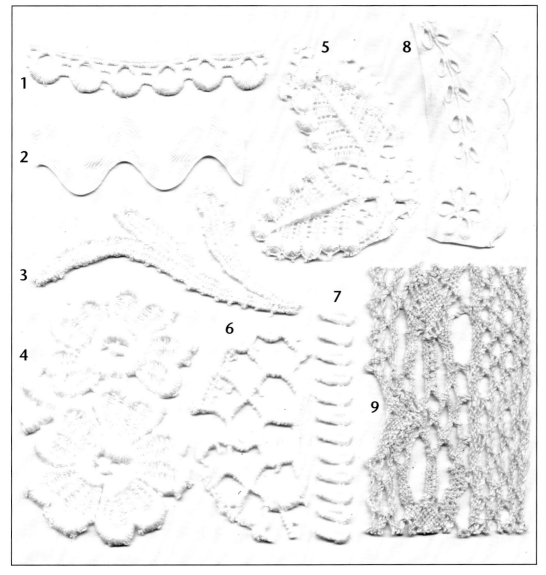

Lace for different uses

Samples 1, 3, 4, 5 and 7 could be cut into sections and arranged to form the suggestion of architectural details

Ricrac (2) can be ruched and manipulated in various ways

Samples 6 and 9 would create wonderful textured surfaces when used as wadding between two other layers

The broderie anglaise (8) would work well for layered edges and collaged motifs

Broderie anglaise flowers

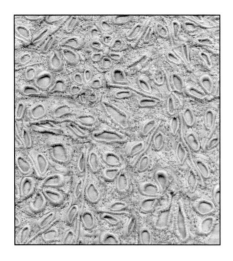

Broderie anglaise edges

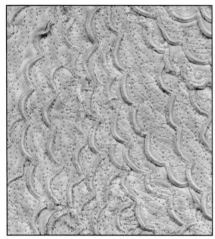

New fabric created by wrapping a frame with threads and fabric strips and stitching randomly across the work

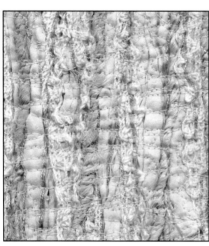

Sandwich of string snippets, stitched randomly between the string pieces

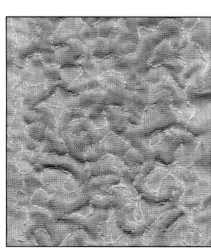

Torn strips

An interesting way of creating a new fabric is to wrap a mixture of torn fabric strips and a variety of threads around a frame, then sew them down by machine. Use a square wire frame made from a coat hanger (**a**) or thick card (**b**), and wrap the materials over the frame from top to bottom, leaving no gaps (**c**). Set your machine up for free machining and place the frame under the foot; stitch randomly all across the work to secure the threads and strips (**d**). When you have finished, cut the newly-made fabric from the frame (**e**).

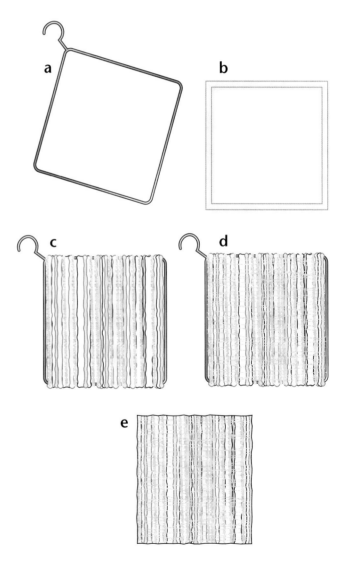

Thick yarn

I made the final sample in this collection by laying snippets of thick cotton string onto a background and securing them with a few stitches. I then covered the whole piece with a very thin cotton fabric, and machined all over using a vermicelli-type pattern. This produces a smooth, embossed surface which can be dry-brushed with extra colour to emphasise the texture.

Old cotton pillow cases and tablecloths that have been washed many times have a soft and drapey quality that is excellent for embroidery and manipulation.

Machined lace samples
In samples 1, 2, 3 and 4 I've cut lace into pieces, rearranged them, and stitched them down onto various backgrounds

Cotton velvet and machined lace
For samples 5 and 6, I laid small lace elements onto cotton velvet and stitched them down with free machining

1

2
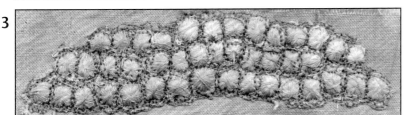

3
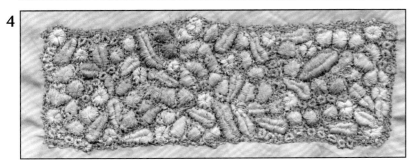

4
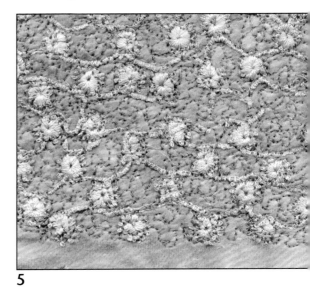

5
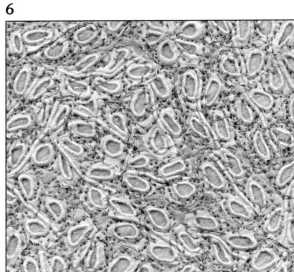

6

Machine Patterns

Even if you only have a few stitch patterns on your sewing machine, they can be very useful if you work with them creatively. For most of these techniques I recommend a firm ground fabric such as calico.

Experiment using different patterns on top of previous lines of stitching, or encroach on the edges of previous lines. You can also make short runs of patterns in different directions. Individual stitches or motifs can be stitched in various directions; do these after, and on top of, the base stitches. It will take some time to build up a surface so that very little of the ground fabric shows through. Try shiny and matt threads, too, which add extra interest.

Another interesting technique is to stretch loose cotton scrim firmly in a frame, then stitch across it with a wide satin stitch; the stitching will gather the fabric to form veins running down the work. Meander randomly over the fabric to create the effect you're looking for.

Machined patterns

1 Daisy stitch worked on muslin
2 Various machine patterns stitched onto calico
3 Freehand satin stitch on scrim

1

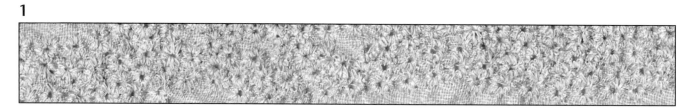

2

3

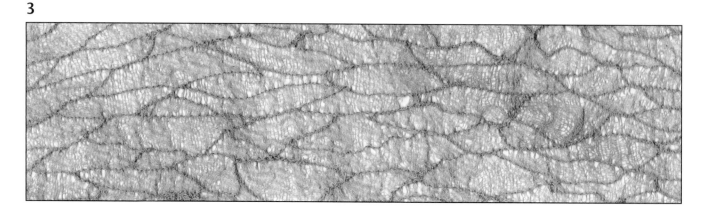

Creating Texture using a Soluble Sandwich

Begin with heavy cotton lace and/or crochet, and cut it into small sections – ignoring any design on the lace as we're only interested in the texture. Working with a heavy transparent soluble film (or any other soluble fabric that you like using), lay small snippets over the surface; these should butt up against each other leaving no gaps, but not overlap. Cover with another layer of soluble film; this can be fine or heavy, but preferably should be transparent. Pin all across the work to secure the layers. Set your machine up for free machining and a wide zigzag, and gently stitch all across the work; then remove the pins, and stitch all over at random, turning the piece as you work. Don't stitch too densely, as the stitching is just to hold the pieces together to form a new fabric.

When you think you've stitched everything, hold the work up to the light to check that you have connected all the pieces – you want to ensure that the new fabric will hold together once the film is washed away. Once you're happy, dissolve the film in warm water and lay the new fabric out to dry.

Instead of using lace, you can also sandwich small snippets of muslin, scrim or silk between two pieces of soluble film; then machine as described above. This creates a thinner final fabric which, once you've dissolved the soluble layers, can be used for manipulation. With both these techniques the fabrics and threads should all be natural, but they will still take up any dye differently.

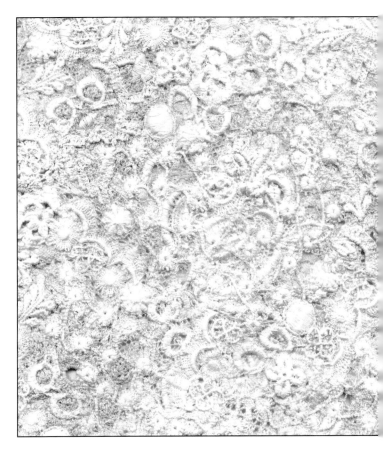

Fabrics created using soluble sandwiches

Lace scraps joined to make a new fabric (above)

A rough surface texture (below); small scraps of heavier fabric, yarns and lace laid on a thin base fabric, and machined all over randomly with a wide satin stitch

Using Lace or Crochet as Wadding

Lace as wadding

For these three samples I used different weights and patterns of lace as a wadding underneath a fine top fabric; freehand machine stitching meanders across the surface.

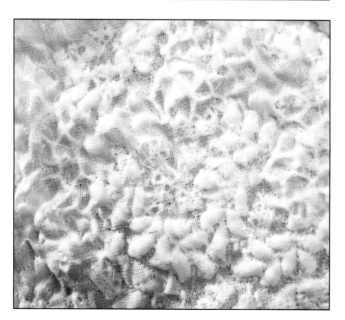

Old household linens such as chair-backs, table runners and table mats often have heavy lace or crochet edgings which can add an extra dimension to your surfaces if used as wadding. Start with a cotton or calico ground/base fabric, and a very fine fabric such as cotton lawn, closely-woven muslin or turban cotton for the top layer. This way, the thin top fabric will take on the shape and texture of the 'wadding,' creating an embossed surface.

Cut the lace and/or crochet into small pieces, ignoring the designs, and place them on the ground fabric; they should butt up tightly, with no gaps between the pieces. Pin the pieces down and very lightly machine-tack across the work, just enough to keep the scraps in place when the pins are taken out. Remove the pins and place the fine fabric on top.

Set your sewing machine up for free machining. Starting in the centre and working outwards, stitch all across the work evenly with small vermicelli-type movements. Work slowly, so that the stitches stay small but the work is not too densely sewn. The finished work will have a smooth surface embossed with the designs of the lace/crochet. To add textures, you can work hand stitching such as seeding, French knots or fly stitch on top.

Architectural Features

Moroccan architecture

You can also 'fussy-cut' lace or crochet motifs and arrange them to make a design of your choice. This lends itself well to architectural features such as doors, windows, arches and carved stone. The lace can either be on top of the fabric or used as wadding.

For the pieces shown here I cut thick cotton lace motifs into smaller sections and collaged them to create the suggestion of windows, arches and carved stone. Each lace collage was tacked into place on a calico base fabric, then covered with a fine cotton fabric; I then free machined around the different features to create an embossed effect.

Moroccan architecture
These four embroideries use heavy cotton lace as wadding. I cut up the lace and collaged the pieces to suggest windows and carvings, and then laid a fine piece of fabric over the top; once I'd stitched round the motifs, I painted the piece with dyes.

Embossed details

My inspiration for this piece came from the carved stones of Ephesus, Turkey. I completed the work in white, then painted it with dyes; finally I highlighted the motifs using a white gel pen.

Layering Fabrics

If you want to create a strata-like effect where many layers of different soils and gravel have formed cliffs, strips of fabrics and machining can be very effective.

Begin with strips of different natural fabrics in white and cream; these could be muslin, scrim, lawn, silks or cottons. Cut the edges of the strips in wavy lines; make some of the strips shorter or thinner if you wish. Arrange the strips in a random fashion onto a calico or cotton ground; think of making them resemble rock formations, using alternate tones and textures of fabric. (Some strips could have slits made in them, to reveal the fabrics underneath.)

Using a white or cream cotton thread, machine over the edges of the strips, to hold them down and merge them into each other. Use whatever automatic patterns you have on your machine, especially if they look organic; change the pattern frequently. Short bursts of patterns on different levels, and individual stitched motifs, can be scattered over the piece – as you stitch, keep in mind the direction in which the strata are going. You can also use free machining, working in wavy lines to follow the flow of the strips, or machine in small pieces of lace that have no identifiable pattern to add extra texture.

Hand stitching on top of the work, in a white or cream natural thread, will enrich the texture even more. Try running small sections of seeding, French knots, fly stitch, Cretan stitch and drawn-up running stitches along the fabric throughout the piece. Keep your design source nearby, and refer to it frequently.

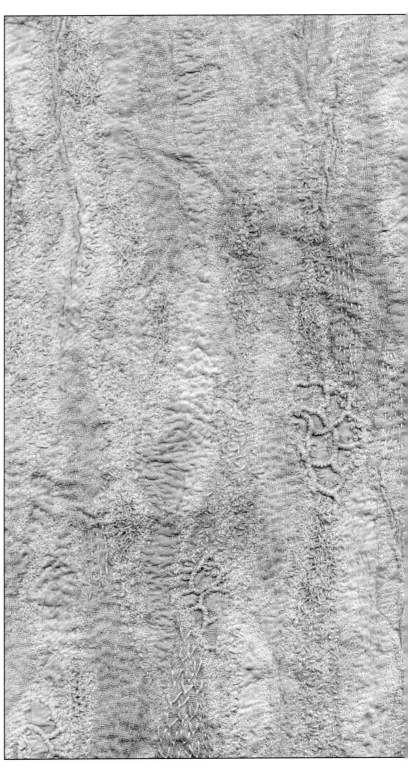

Strata surface

A complex piece formed from strips of many different fabrics, layered and machined, and then embellished with many different styles of hand stitching

Hand Stitching for Texture

Hand stitching adds another dimension to your work, especially when it's done on top of machine stitching, which can often be quite flat. The hand stitches should integrate and blend with any existing texture. Using several close tones in the same colour will add interest. Hand stitches can meander through several background textures and help to integrate them; they should never stand out as if they've been added as an afterthought. You'll find it useful – and a spur to your creativity – if you have a good stitch dictionary to hand for reference, but here are just a few ideas.

Threads

It adds interest to your work if you use a variety of threads such as cotton perlé, stranded cotton, crochet cotton, soft cotton, coton à broder, silk and linen. Some of these (such as cotton perlé) come in various thicknesses, and each thread has its own finish: matt or shiny, rough or smooth.

Running stitch

Lines of running stitch worked across the piece can be drawn up to create ripples in the fabric. Horizontal lines of running stitch make vertical ripples, and vice versa. It can also look really good if you work small sections in different directions.

Hand embroidery stitches

1 For this piece I started with a loosely-woven fabric, and oversewed sections to pull the fabric into holes. Once I'd layered the work with other fabrics, I then added French knots.

2 This sample of hand stitches was worked with threads of various thicknesses; I only used straight stitches, but worked them in lots of different directions.

1

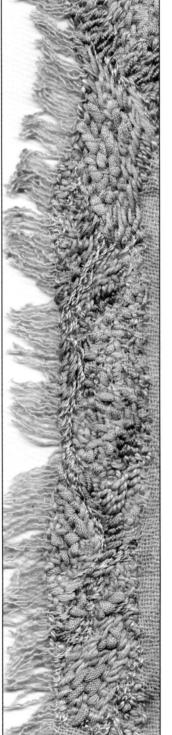

2

Seeding stitch

Seeding consists of very short stitches worked closely in different directions. They can be heaped on top of each other to create a denser texture.

Cross stitches

Try working random cross stitches on your work; these can be piled on top of each other, perhaps worked in different threads, for a dense texture.

Velvet stitch

This lesser-known stitch creates a looped pile.

French knots and colonial knots

Embroidered knots can be done in a variety of thicknesses of thread; you can also vary the size of the finished knot by altering the number of times you wind the thread around the needle. A variety of threads and knot sizes produces an interesting surface; place the knots tightly together, or scatter them as required.

Needle-weaving

Detached knotted buttonhole stitch is just one of many stitches you can explore for needle-weaving; there are many others. Internet searches will reveal all kinds of ideas, from simple to complex.

Fly stitch, Cretan stitch, bullion knots and knot stitch

All of these can be very effective when stitched randomly and creatively across your work.

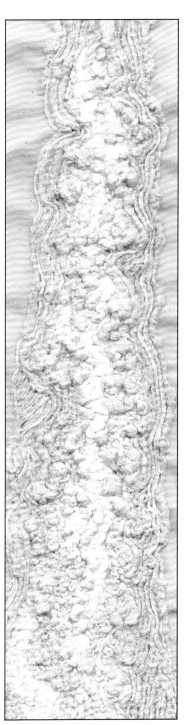

Mixed applied yarns

On these two samples I knotted and couched down various yarns, then added French knots; you can see how different pieces look before and after tea-dyeing.

Hand embroidery

*Running stitch, satin stitch
and seeding, worked in various
thicknesses of thread, created
this embellished surface*

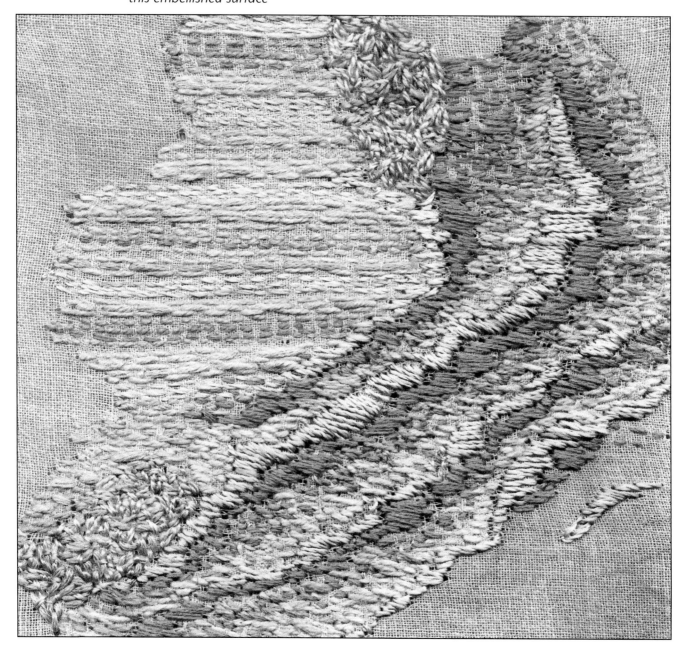

Contemporary Textured Surfaces

Fault Line *vessel*
30cm (h) x 13cm (w)

Mixed Surface Textures

You can create a very interesting surface texture by using a variety of fabric scraps and integrating them with various machine-stitched patterns. When the piece is dyed, the fabrics will take up the colour in different intensities, producing a variety of tones in the work. Silk usually produces a stronger tone, so make sure that the different fabrics are spread evenly over the work.

1 On a medium-weight ground fabric, lay scraps of natural fabrics in white and cream. The scraps should be quite small and could include fine cotton lace, crochet lace, cotton threads, silk, cotton, muslin or any natural fabric scraps.

2 Pin the pieces, then meander across the surface with free machining just enough to hold the fabrics in place; remove the pins.

3 Using white and cream cotton machine thread alternately, free machine across the surface to secure the patches. You want the texture of the finished piece to look organic, so work in short bursts in different directions, and meander randomly across the work with no long straight lines.

4 Set your machine back to ordinary stitching, and use any of your machine patterns that seem suitable – for instance daisies, stars, ovals, and short runs of border patterns. Use white thread on cream fabric and cream thread on white fabric. Your aim is to disguise completely the edges of the scraps, and to integrate the patches visually. If you wish, you can add hand stitching either before or after dyeing.

Mixed surface

I used a variety of natural fabrics and fibres in white and cream, and machined them onto a ground fabric.

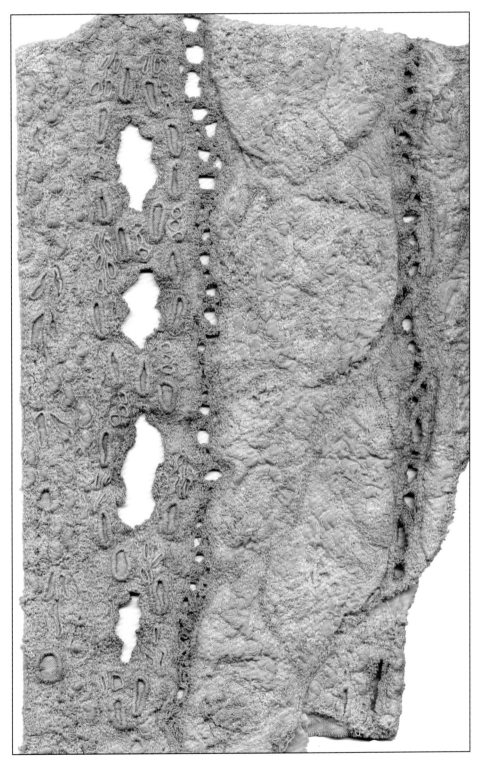

Mixed surface techniques

In this sample I began by free machining scraps of broderie anglaise and satin-stitched lace onto soluble fabric. I left holes deliberately, edging them with machine stitching for added interest. A line of faggoting of varied width runs the length of the work. I quilted the next section using scraps of lace as wadding; solid machined lines break up the large area, then another line of faggoting.

The whole piece was worked onto soluble fabric, then I dissolved the fabric and tea-dyed the final piece: all the techniques are included in the book.

Mixed surface textures

Various natural fabrics, plus thick fibres in white and cream, machined onto a ground fabric; I incorporated dark lace edges to add interest.

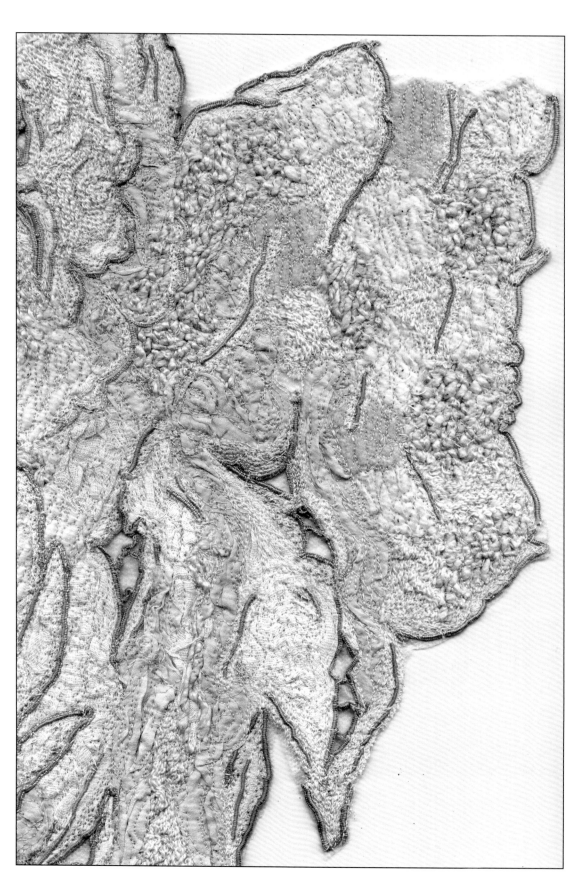

Tea-Dyeing

Most of my work is tea-dyed, and it is fairly simple to do; I use a large, square lasagne dish, but any similar vessel will do. Put in about six teabags, and pour over boiling water. Then immerse the fabric for a few minutes, squeeze it, and put it to dry. The number of teabags and the amount of water you use will make a difference in tone. Either leave the teabags in the dish, or remove them when the colour has drained out of them. Ideally you want to dry the work flat, naturally (ie, not using a hairdryer etc), overnight. If your fabric is thin and you leave it crumpled as it dries, this can create an attractive effect as a stronger colour will accumulate in the creases.

The fabric will lighten slightly as it dries. If the colour is darker than you want, rinse the work in water to make it paler, then re-dye it. However, even when you're using different fabrics stitched together sometimes the resulting tone of colour is very even. When a piece of textured work is dyed and dry, I make a stronger dye solution with one or two teabags in a half cup of boiling water. When this has cooled I squeeze the teabag fairly dry, and lightly touch the top of the fabric texture. This creates a contrast, and highlights the textures in a stronger variety of tones. Once this has dried in turn, you can repeat the process to darken some areas even more and give still more depth to the work.

You can dye your work when it's complete, or you can dye the fabrics separately before work begins. This can result in a more visually lively work as the separately-dyed fabrics may vary considerably more in tone.

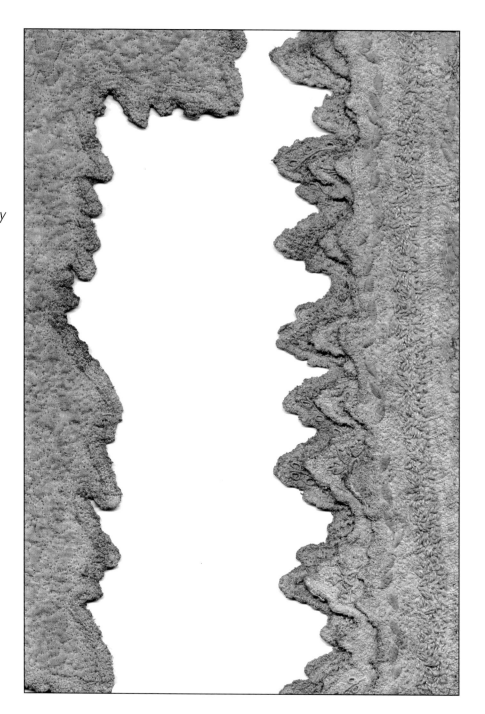

Decorative edges

To create the edges of this example, I positioned a strip of soluble fabric under the edge of my work and pinned it in place. (I did this before it was dyed, because the soluble fabric needs to be washed away.) I then free machined along the edge of the fabric to seal the fabric layers together, and extended the free stitching out onto the soluble fabric. You can create different styles of edges according to how you work the stitches. Picots or circles extended over the edge of the fabric need stitching over several times, to ensure that they stay firm when the soluble film is washed away.

Edges

The edges of your work are very important, and should be considered right from the start. They should be in keeping with the rest of the piece, and suitable for the ultimate purpose – for instance, bear in mind whether you want to frame your finished piece, build it into a 3D structure etc. Suitable edges will help the piece to hang or sit properly, and enhance the whole item without drawing attention away from the textile work.

One way of creating a finish is to stitch a fine cord to the edge of the work by hand or machine, using a wide satin stitch. Various machine patterns can be used along or over the edges of the work. Several hand embroidery stitches are suitable for creating edges: blanket stitch, braid edging and looped edging work well – also various stitches with picots (little loops).

Contemporary Textured Surfaces

Suggestions for Further Work

Ideas and experiments

Try some of these ideas and see how you like the effects, and how you can vary them; you'll then have a whole 'library' of different ideas you can incorporate into your future work.

1 Use stretchy fabric such as cotton jersey, and machine along the edge with satin stitch while stretching the fabric. This will form a curled edge. Short lengths can be cut and applied to a ground fabric.

2 Create cloth by machining on soluble fabric, with or without the addition of fabric scraps. Small sections can be curled and layered onto a ground fabric.

3 Stitch on top of loose cotton knitting or crochet by hand or machine, drawing the threads together to make various-sized holes.

4 Yarns that are too thick or knobbly to sew with can be couched down on the top of the fabric with a finer thread.

5 Make lots of cords in different gauges for intertwining like tree roots. Fill gaps between the cords with ruching or knotted hand stitching.

6 Lumpy/textured yarns can be laid down and stitched over with decorative hand stitching.

7 Layer three different tones of textured fabric and machine the layers together. Cut through the upper layer between the stitching, and also cut through the top two layers in places to reveal the different fabrics.

8 Lay smooth fine fabric over parts of a texture so that some areas are smoother.

9 Textured fabric can be manipulated several times more to achieve a complex and interesting surface; this will result in a sturdier fabric.

10 Make small running stitches across an already textured surface. Do this again in a different direction to the previous stitches and draw up the thread slightly as you work – this will create an extra dimension.

11 Wadding can be used as padding in small areas. Use two layers of fabric and outline the area to be padded with stitching. The wadding can be pushed through a slit in the back of the under layer, and the slit then sewn up. (This is one version of what's sometimes called trapunto quilting.)

12 Collages of fabric and lace can be added on top of work, or you can cut holes cut to create apertures, to add more interest to the work.

13 Scrunch up a piece of fine fabric and secure it with stab stitches to a thicker ground fabric. Sometimes textures such as this will give you inspiration for a completely new design.

14 Finely pleat a piece of fabric, leaving the pleats to stand up proud. Cords can be laid between the pleats and couched down.

15 Sew cords together in a creative way, leaving spaces or loops between the joinings.

16 If you're not happy with a composition, cut it up, seal the edges and faggot the pieces back together – or use them for collage.

17 Experiment with cutting strips of different fabrics (use different thicknesses too), then twist or plait them and sew them down on your work.

18 Lastly, just relax and enjoy the processes of scrunching, rolling, twisting, wrapping and gathering.

Folds of Time *vessels*

both 43cm (h) x 10cm (w)

The vessel on the left features random pleating and fabric manipulation, achieved by pinching and securing the fabric to create an organic appearance. The one on the right shows a section of machine faggoting edged with ruching, running from the top to the bottom.

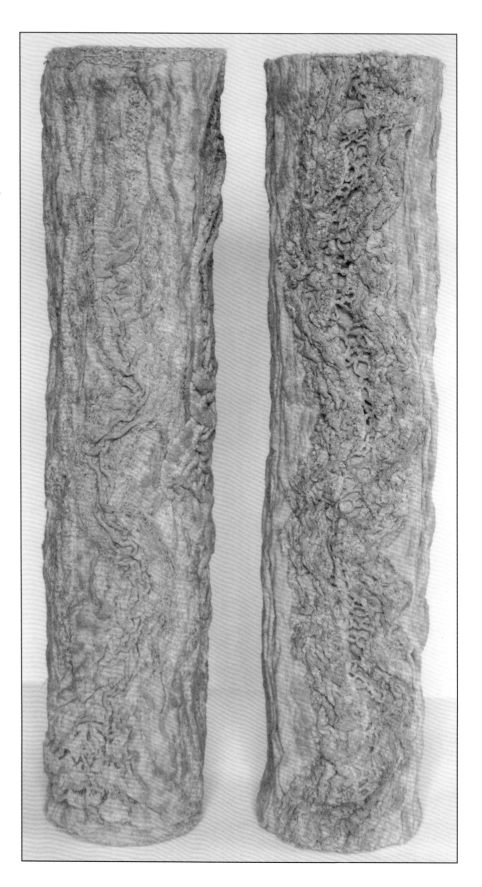

Faggoted vessel, **Folds of Time**
30cm (h) x 15cm (w)
I inserted machine faggoting into this vessel to create a focal point.

Cave *front view*

16cm (h) x 16cm (w)

This work includes rough and smooth textures, combined with a variety of pleating styles and fabric manipulation.

Cave *side view*

Cave 2 *front view*
21cm (h) x 19cm (w)

I created a quilted fabric for the top, using lace as wadding to create texture, and the piece also features couched cords and beads.

Cave 2 *rear view*

Cliff Face *vessel*

26cm (h) x 21cm (w)

The centre section shows a variety of couched cords and folded fabrics, with clusters of beads that were inserted afterwards; this is surrounded by gathered, textured fabrics.

Cliff *20cm (h) x 33cm (w)*

The top ridge was created from scraps of lace machined onto soluble fabric. The middle ridge is a combination of manipulated ricrac, couched cords and folded lace strips; this is supported by random gathering set on a quilted base.

Rock Climb *view*

20cm (h) x 16cm (w)

A machine quilted fabric was cut into sections which were folded and hand stitched to hold the shapes together.

Petrified Trees

*large 30cm (h) x 9cm (w);
medium 25cm (h) x 14cm (w);
small 15cm (h) x 6cm (w)*

*The three petrified trees
were made from different
weights of ribbed silk
fabric. I collaged small
sections of fabric onto
soluble fabric, then pushed
the fabric into ridges and
machined them to hold
the shape. I deliberately
left holes, and then
oversewed the edges
with hand stitching.*

Gargoyle

40cm (h) x 30cm (w)

I cut the base for this Gargoyle from carpet felt, and roughly tacked and oversewed it with large stitches to hold its shape. I then constructed a top fabric with scraps of fabrics and threads, machined heavily onto a soluble fabric base.

I used many different shades of grey, brown and green, blended together with machine zigzag stitch in brown, green and grey threads. After I'd washed the fabric, I applied it onto the shaped base, securing it with hand stitching.

A Cenote 20cm (h) x 32cm (w)

A Cenote (say-NO-tay) is a natural sinkhole resulting from the collapse of limestone bedrock which exposes groundwater underneath, especially associated with the Yucatán Peninsula of Mexico. Tree roots intertwine with rocks that have worn smooth from the waterflow.

A variety of textures were needed to complete this piece.